Philadelphia

Philadelphia

A Downtown America Book

Bernadette Balcer and Fran O'Byrne-Pelham

Dillon Press
New York

Collier Macmillan Canada
Toronto

Maxwell Macmillan International Publishing Group
New York   Oxford   Singapore   Sydney

To the Children of America

Library of Congress Cataloging-in-Publication Data

Balcer, Bernadette.
Philadelphia / by Bernadette Balcer and Fran O'Byrne-Pelham.
(A Downtown America book)
Includes index.
Summary: Describes the past and present, neighborhoods, historic sites, attractions, and festivals of Philadelphia.
1. Philadelphia (Pa.)—Juvenile literature. [1. Philadelphia (Pa.)] I. O'Byrne-Pelham, Fran. II. Title. III. Series.
F158.33.B35 1989   974.8'11   88-20198
ISBN 0-87518-388-3

Macmillan Publishing Company, 866 Third Avenue
New York, NY 10022

Printed in the United States of America
  2 3 4 5 6 7 8 9 10

Acknowledgments

We wish to thank the Philadelphia children who helped us as we worked on this book. A special thanks to Marianne Bucci, librarian at the Fox Chase Branch of the Free Library of Philadelphia, and to Anne Robinson of City Councilman Brian O'Neill's office. We would also like to thank the librarians at the Jenkintown Library, Susan Oates of the Philadelphia Convention and Visitor's Bureau, and the public relations people from the stations KYW and WPVI. Finally, thanks to our editor, Tom Schneider, and to Pat, Patrick, and Sarah Balcer, and Don, Mary, and Michael Pelham.

The photographs are reproduced through the courtesy of Terry Burns; Marc Daniels; Delaware Division, Port Authority; Deng Jeng Lee; KYW-TV; Pennsylvania Division of Travel Marketing; Philadelphia Civic Center Museum; Philadelphia Convention and Visitor's Bureau; Philadelphia Museum of Art; Philadelphia Zoo; and WPVI TV.

Contents

Fast Facts about Philadelphia

Philadelphia: City of Brotherly Love, Quaker City, Cradle of Liberty

Location: Middle Atlantic, southeastern corner of Pennsylvania

Area: 144 square miles (373 square kilometers), including 9 square miles (23 square kilometers) of inland water; consolidated metropolitan area, 5,515 square miles (14,284 square kilometers)

Population (1986 estimate*): City, 1,642,900; consolidated metropolitan area, 5,832,600

Major Population Groups: Blacks, Italians, Irish, Germans, Polish, Russians, Puerto Ricans, English

Altitude: Highest, 431 feet (131 meters) above sea level; lowest, sea level

Climate: Average temperature is 35°F (2°C) in January, 76°F (24°C) in July; average annual precipitation, including rain and snow, is 43 inches (109 centimeters)

Founding Date: 1682, chartered as a city in 1701

City Flag: Two vertical blue stripes on either side of a yellow stripe bearing the city seal

City Seal: A coat of arms supported by two women; above it, a right arm holds a pair of scales, and beneath it is the city's motto "Philadelphia Maneto" ("Let Brotherly Love Continue")

Form of Government: A mayor governs the city, along with the 17-member city council (which makes the city laws). All are elected to serve four-year terms.

Important Industries: Clothing, oil refining, processed foods, chemicals, paper products

*U.S. Bureau of the Census 1988 population estimates available in fall 1989; official 1990 census figures available in 1991-92.

Festivals and Parades

January: New Year's Day Mummers' Parade

March: St. Patrick's Day Parade

April: Easter Parade

May: Jambalaya Jam, Cajun Food Festival

June: Greek Festival; Jazz Festival

July: Freedom Festival; Hispanic Festival; Afro-American Festival; Red, White, and Blue Festival

August: German Festival; Polish Festival

September: Rock 'A' Rama Rock and Roll Festival

October: Columbus Day Parade; Super Sunday

November: Thanksgiving Day Parade

For further information about festivals and parades, see agencies listed on page 56.

United States

CANADA

Seattle
Olympia
WASHINGTON
Portland
Salem
OREGON
Boise
IDAHO

MONTANA
Helena

NORTH DAKOTA
Bismarck

Lake Superior

MINNESOTA
St. Paul
WISCONSIN
Minneapolis
Madison
Milwaukee
Lansing
Lake Huron
Lake Michigan
MICHIGAN
Detroit
Lake Ontario
Lake Erie

NEW HAMPSHIRE
VERMONT
MAINE
Montpelier
Augusta
Concord
MASSACHUSE
Albany
Boston
Providence
NEW YORK
Hartford
RHODE ISLA
CONNECTICUT

SOUTH DAKOTA
Pierre

WYOMING

Great Salt Lake
Salt Lake City

Sacramento
Carson City
San Francisco
NEVADA

CALIFORNIA

UTAH
Las Vegas
Los Angeles
San Diego
ARIZONA
Phoenix
Tucson

Cheyenne

Denver

COLORADO

Albuquerque
Santa Fe
NEW MEXICO
El Paso

NEBRASKA
Lincoln
Omaha

KANSAS
Topeka

Des Moines
IOWA

Chicago
ILLINOIS
Springfield

Kansas City
Jefferson City
St. Louis
MISSOURI

Mississippi

INDIANA
Indianapolis

OHIO
Columbus
Cincinnati

PENNSYLVANIA
Pittsburgh
Harrisburg
Cleveland

WEST VIRGINIA
Frankfort
Charleston
KENTUCKY
Louisville

Trenton
New York City
Philadelphia
NEW JERSEY
Dover
DELAWARE
Baltimore
Annapolis
Washington, D.C.
MARYLAND
Richmond
VIRGINIA

Nashville
TENNESSEE
Memphis

Tulsa
Oklahoma City
OKLAHOMA

Little Rock
ARKANSAS

Raleigh
NORTH CAROLINA
Charlotte
Columbia
SOUTH CAROLINA

Birmingham
Atlanta
GEORGIA

MEXICO

Fort Worth
Dallas

TEXAS

San Antonio
Austin
Houston

Rio Grande

LOUISIANA
Jackson
MISSISSIPPI
ALABAMA
Montgomery
Baton Rouge
New Orleans

Jacksonville
Tallahassee

FLORIDA
St. Petersburg
Tampa

Miami

Gulf of Mexico

Pacific Ocean

Atlantic Ocean

U.S.S.R.

ALASKA
Anchorage

CANADA

Honolulu
Juneau

HAWAII

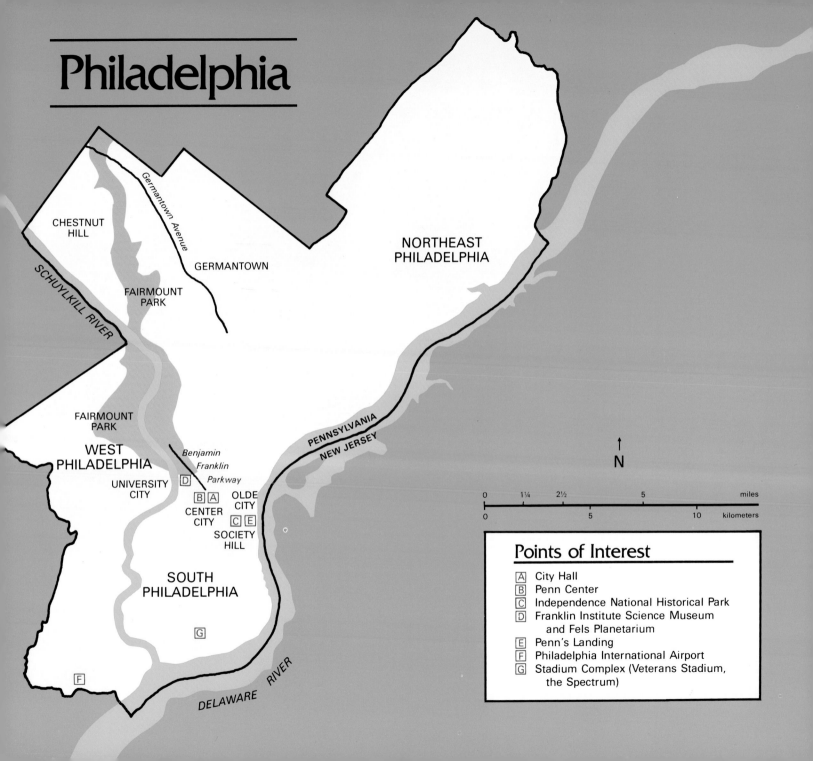

Philadelphia

CHESTNUT
HILL

Germantown Avenue

GERMANTOWN

FAIRMOUNT
PARK

SCHUYLKILL RIVER

NORTHEAST
PHILADELPHIA

FAIRMOUNT
PARK

WEST
PHILADELPHIA

*Benjamin
Franklin
Parkway*

UNIVERSITY
CITY

D

B A

CENTER
CITY

OLDE
CITY

C E

SOCIETY
HILL

SOUTH
PHILADELPHIA

G

F

PENNSYLVANIA

NEW JERSEY

DELAWARE RIVER

N

0	1¼	2½	5	miles
0		5	10	kilometers

Points of Interest

A City Hall
B Penn Center
C Independence National Historical Park
D Franklin Institute Science Museum
   and Fels Planetarium
E Penn's Landing
F Philadelphia International Airport
G Stadium Complex (Veterans Stadium,
   the Spectrum)

1

Welcome to Philadelphia:

From high above City Hall courtyard, a statue of William Penn watches over Philadelphia. If you could stand on top of the statue, in the rim of Penn's hat, you would see that his city stretches for miles in every direction. Looking down, you would see the blocks of row houses that line the streets. You would see train tracks criss-crossing under two expressways that lead into and out of Philadelphia.

But you would not see the subway trains that run beneath the city.

William Penn received a charter from King Charles II of England more than three centuries ago to establish the colony of Pennsylvania. In 1682, Penn sailed up the Delaware River to his new settlement. According to a legend, Penn jumped off his ship, the *Welcome*, and danced for joy on the river bank. As a Quaker (a member

The statue of William Penn *(center)* rises above the City Hall courtyard in the heart of downtown Philadelphia.

At a festival at Penn's Landing, this young Philadelphian had her face painted.

of a religious group that does not believe in war) he wanted to create a "green countrie towne" that would offer religious freedom to all its citizens. He named the town *Philadelphia*, the Greek word for *brotherly love*.

Today, the spot where he came ashore is called Penn's Landing. There, on Sunday afternoons, crowds gather to listen to the music of rock or reggae bands. On the Fourth of July, people watch sizzling fireworks that light up the ships in the harbor. Sometimes, tall ships, sailing in from

An old-fashioned tall ship at Penn's Landing.

Row houses and shops line Philadelphia's Headhouse Square.

faraway lands, attract thousands of Philadelphians to the docks.

When Penn arrived in Philadelphia, he found a small community of about 200 settlers. Now, more than 1.6 million people live in the city.

The streets and homes of Philadel-phia have changed, too. The people in the city no longer live in log cabins, wigwams, and caves as the first settlers did. Now, most Philadelphians live in row houses—two or three-story houses that share at least one wall with the house next door. In some parts of Philadelphia, row houses line entire streets.

Today, big buildings crowd the center of Philadelphia, and the skyline keeps changing. Near City Hall, the bank and office buildings of Penn Center cover three downtown blocks. Until 1987, the statue of William Penn towered over the city's buildings, 548 feet (167 meters) above the ground. In that year, a giant skyscraper, covered in mirrored glass, rose taller than William Penn.

Philadelphia, the fifth largest city in America, is a blend of the new and the old. Every day, construction teams are hard at work on superhighways, shopping malls, and skyscrapers. Gleaming new hotels in and around the city host business people

Looking out from City Hall, the tall buildings of Center City rise along the Benjamin Franklin Parkway.

and doctors at meetings. In the last few years, crews from Hollywood have set up their cameras to film *Rocky* and other movies on Philadelphia's streets.

Philadelphia lies on the East Coast between two other big cities—New York City and Washington, D.C. It is in the southeastern corner of Pennsylvania, beside the Delaware River. The river, which flows into the Atlantic Ocean, makes Philadelphia an excellent port. Four bridges cross the river and connect the city with New Jersey. On hot summer days, Philadelphians pack up their station wagons and cross those bridges on the way to the Jersey shore.

The weather is often on the minds of Philadelphians. They talk about it all the time. Mostly, they complain that it's too hot, too cold, too rainy, or too snowy. Actually, Philadelphia seasons are quite pleasant. Snow on the rock ledges along Kelly Drive melts in time for the cherry trees to blossom in spring. When summer sizzles, children in the city cool themselves under the spray of curbside fire hydrants. In the fall, oak, maple, and chestnut trees drop brightly colored leaves.

In Philadelphia, people can sail or canoe down the Schuylkill River, or take boat rides down the Delaware. In the city's many museums, they can touch dinosaur bones or trace fossil prints. Every week, the *Philadelphia Inquirer* lists puppet shows, pet shows, plays, and nature

Sailing on the Schuylkill River is a favorite activity for Philadelphians.

hikes. Many of these activities take place near the city's bustling center.

Around City Hall, Philadelphia buzzes with activity. City government, under the mayor and city council, is conducted in the blue and gray building which looks like an old French castle. Stone gargoyles, perched on the edges of the building, stick their tongues out at people on the sidewalk below.

Each day, thousands of people pack into silver trains and red and white buses on the way to their jobs in downtown Philadelphia. Insurance companies, chemical companies, law offices, and banks fill the downtown area. The first bank in the country was built in Philadelphia, and the city has long been a center of commerce and industry. It is now the fifth largest industrial center in the United States.

Philadelphia companies produce many useful products, ranging from clothing and packaged foods to refined oil and medicines. The first computer, a huge machine called ENIAC, was created at the University of Pennsylvania. Some delicious treats were first discovered in Philadelphia, too. Bubble gum was invented in the city, and the Fleer factory still wraps the chewy pink stuff in Philadelphia. A young medical student brewed the first root beer here in 1866. Philadelphians also claim to have discovered ice cream. Dolly Madison, who made ice cream a well-known dessert, took her recipe to the White House when she left Philadelphia.

Since Dolly Madison's time, millions of immigrants have come to Philadelphia because of the freedom and opportunity William Penn's city offered. During the mid-1800s, the city welcomed large numbers of families from England, Ireland, Germany, Scotland, and Wales. Later, in the early 1900s, many thousands arrived from Italy, Poland, Austria, Hungary, and Russia. Recently, Asian refugees, fleeing war in their countries, found shelter in Philadelphia.

During the period before the Civil War, Philadelphia Quakers like Lucretia Mott opened their doors to blacks fleeing slavery. Black Americans arrived in Philadelphia by the thousands during and after World War II to fill jobs in the city's growing

Boys and girls enjoy a food Philadelphia is known for—Philly pretzels.

Young black Philadelphians skipping rope in Germantown.

industries. Today, about four of every ten Philadelphians are black—the largest single group in the city.

William Penn's settlement is now a modern city. Downtown Philadelphia is called Center City. Within Center City lies the Olde City, a fa-

mous historical area. From Center City, Philadelphia spreads out into 110 different neighborhoods. Some have names that refer to old homes in England, such as Olney, Kensington, and Port Richmond. Other neighborhoods, such as Germantown and Chinatown, are named after their settlers. Still other neighborhoods—Juniata, Manayunk, and Wissahickon—have kept their American Indian names.

Philadelphia is a city with an important past. On July 4, 1776, members of the Second Continental Congress adopted the Declaration of Independence in what is now Independence Hall. In 1787, delegates from all over the United States came to the city to write the U.S. Constitution. From 1790 to 1800, Philadelphia served as the capital of the new nation. During part of that time, George Washington and his wife Martha lived here.

For Americans, Philadelphia's historic places are so important that the U.S. government helped restore them during the 1950s and 1960s. Today, visitors from near and far come to the Cradle of Liberty city to learn about the birth of a great nation—the United States of America.

2

The Magic of Center City

Postcards from Philadelphia often picture Independence Hall or the Liberty Bell. Both of these famous monuments are located in Independence National Historical Park, which is part of Philadelphia's Olde City.

The buildings in the Olde City are neat and well kept. Americans treasure the Graff House, where Thomas Jefferson wrote the Declaration of Independence, Carpenters' Hall, where the First Continental Congress met, and Independence Hall, where the Constitution was signed. In the 1940s, these historic buildings and the houses around them were crumbling. The United States government decided to help restore the historic buildings for everyone to enjoy. The old houses were restored, too, and are now part of a beautiful neighborhood called Society Hill.

Independence Hall in Independence National Historical Park.

Every day of the year, people tread the cobblestone streets of the Olde City. Some visitors ride in horse-drawn carriages to explore the famous streets. They usually stop in front of Independence Hall. This red brick building looks much like it did in 1776, when men in powdered wigs met there to sign the Declaration of Independence.

A 2,000-pound (909-kilogram) bronze bell, the Liberty Bell, once pealed in the tower of Independence Hall. People who visit the bell hear the story of how it chimed all through the night when the Declaration of Independence was read to the public. They listen to a park ranger tell how the bell used to be taken from city to city so that people could see it.

The Liberty Bell at night.

Because it is such a treasure, the bell now rests in a special glass pavilion. All year long, day and night, people can stand and admire it.

Yellow buses filled with schoolchildren roll through old Philadelphia streets each day. Teachers and students often stop at special sites such as the Betsy Ross House on Arch Street. It is said that General George Washington asked Betsy Ross to make the first American flag. In her home, visitors see the shop where she sewed, and the parlor where she met with Washington.

Neither Betsy Ross nor George Washington would recognize Market Street in Olde City. The colonial stalls filled with vegetables, candles, and bolts of linen have been replaced by modern stores. Record stores, shoe stores, and book stores line present-day Market Street. Posters on telephone poles announce boxing matches. Street vendors sell silver jewelry from velvet-covered tables.

Once, merchants along Market Street could wave to Philadelphia's most famous resident, Benjamin Franklin, as he ran from his print shop to his post office to his home. Ben Franklin came to Philadelphia as a teenager, and stayed for seventy years until his death. During his lifetime, he published a well-known almanac and a newspaper. Later, with Thomas Jefferson and other leaders, he helped create the new United States of America. People passing his grave in Olde City often throw pen-

Benjamin Franklin, George Washington, and other famous Americans worshipped at Christ Church.

nies in through the fence for good luck.

In Center City Philadelphia, the name *Franklin* echoes everywhere. Philadelphia has the Franklin Mint, the Franklin Hotel, the Ben Franklin Bridge, and the Ben Franklin Park-

way. Center City also has the Franklin Institute.

Each day children run up the gray stone steps that lead to the Franklin Institute. At this remarkable museum, visitors can inch their way through an 18-foot (5.5-meter) mod-

At night on the Delaware River, lights outline the Benjamin Franklin Bridge and a tall ship at Penn's Landing.

Young people stand next to the Franklin Institute's full-sized locomotive.

el of the human heart, tracing the path of the blood. A museum guide explains that the heart would fit into the body of a human 220 feet (67 meters) tall.

At the Franklin Institute, children can hop aboard a full-sized loco-motive, or climb into the cockpit of a small plane. They take part in experiments with static electricity; young people laugh when the hairs on the head of a volunteer stand straight out. In the planetarium, the audience gazes at stars shining in a black dome.

The huge model of the human heart at the Franklin Institute.

Outside the institute, flags of many nations wave from poles along the Ben Franklin Parkway. The parkway, one of the prettiest streets in Philadelphia, is lined with beautiful buildings and fountains. Here in the spring, yellow and red tulips burst into bloom. Sometimes, Philadelphians sit on the edges of the fountains and munch hot dogs. They may be on their way to the Logan Library to return books, or on their way to the Academy of Natural Sciences to see the stuffed yaks and tigers.

In the space of twenty city blocks, amid the tall buildings and colorful streets of Center City Philadelphia, a number of events take place during the year. For Philadelphians, a favorite event is a parade.

The Mummers' Parade starts each new year. During this colorful celebration, about 16,000 feathered marchers strut down Broad Street strumming their banjos. For hours, crowds stand in crisp winter air behind yellow police barricades to watch the Mummers' String Bands in the city's best-known parade.

When Philadelphia honors a winning sports team, up go the barricades. Down Broad Street march the high school bands, following floats and antique cars.

In 1987, on the two-hundredth anniversary of the U.S. Constitution, visitors from all over the United States joined Philadelphians to watch a spectacular parade on Chestnut Street. In the high buildings, office

Colorful mummers march along Market Street in the Mummers' Parade on New Year's Day.

A giant balloon in Philadelphia's Thanksgiving Day Parade.

workers hung out banners and sprinkled confetti on the colorful marchers.

Each Thanksgiving Day, another parade winds its way through the city streets. At this holiday event, children clutching silver balloons cheer the arrival of Santa Claus.

Parades are not the only events that draw crowds to Center City. Fun-filled festivals attract thousands. The festivals all have a special theme. At the Food Festival, chefs cook up soul food, Greek food, and hot dogs for hungry customers. At the Rock 'A' Rama, dancers boogie on Penn's Landing to the music of rock bands. At the Jambalaya Jam, Philadelphians get a taste of New Orleans food and music.

There's always something going on in Center City Philadelphia. Every day, people with cameras wander in and out of the historic buildings and museums. Commuters hurry to work in department stores, offices, and galleries. Theater goers and music lovers attend plays and concerts. And on special days, Philadelphians go to one of the city's parades or festivals. These exciting events take place on the streets, on Penn's Landing, along the parkway, and in Fairmount Park, the biggest city park in the world.

3

The Biggest City Park in the World

Philadelphians don't need to leave the city to enjoy natural beauty and outdoor activities. In Fairmount Park, bikers pedal along the worn paths beside the Schuylkill River. They may stop to watch teams of scullers who row along the river, their oars moving in perfect time.

Along the Schuylkill banks, picnickers feed geese small pieces of bread crusts. Walkers stroll past the statues and monuments that line the river bank. Fairmount Park has hundreds of statues—of cowboys and generals, saints and presidents, and dancing angels. Horseback riders and hikers follow the park's winding trails.

A million people head for Fairmount Park on a Sunday in October, called Super Sunday. This event is Philadelphia's idea of a street fair. Boys in denim jackets, girls with long

Scullers row in the Schuylkill River.

The Philadelphia Museum of Art.

earrings, mothers and fathers with babies and cameras, older people arm-in-arm—all meet at the entrance to Fairmount Park on that day. While puppeteers put on shows for small children, young singers entertain teenagers. Vendors wave baseball cards. Pizza makers toss dough high into the air, and bakers dip batter into hot oil to make funnel cakes.

The Super Sunday fair is held in front of the most beautiful building in the city, the Philadelphia Museum of Art. The art museum is easy to spot.

It looks like a Greek temple with ninety-nine steps! Giant pillars hold up the blue-tiled roof.

Inside the museum, life-size suits of armor stand guard at one doorway. Giant Buddha statues sit cross-legged in a great hall. A huge painting shows a warrior gripping the reins of his frightened horse. Thousands of paintings hang on the white walls of the art museum. Some visitors spend a whole day just looking at them. They may come back another day to admire the rooms from an ancient temple, an old Spanish courtyard, and a medieval chapel.

Every day, green and red trolleys run by the museum on their trips down the Ben Franklin Parkway. These old-time trolleys carry sight-

Children and their parents enjoy a painting lesson at the art museum.

seers around Center City and through Fairmount Park. People catch the trolley to visit the famous park mansions.

During the Revolutionary War, Benedict Arnold bought one of these mansions, Mount Pleasant, as a wedding present for his beautiful new bride, Peggy Shippen. But Arnold betrayed his country and was arrested and hanged before he ever moved into the huge home. Like the other park mansions, Mount Pleasant is filled with handmade furniture from Philadelphia cabinet makers.

One of the biggest attractions in Fairmount Park is the zoo. Before the Civil War, the United States had no zoo. Some children never saw a wild animal, unless they happened to see a bear in a traveling side show. The Phil-

adelphia Zoo was the first of its kind in the United States. When it opened in 1874, visitors could see first-hand the wonders of a grizzly bear from the West or a tiger from India.

The Philadelphia Zoo is more than a place to go to see animals in cages. It is also a place where young people learn about animal homes, smells, sounds, and behavior.

At the Treehouse, a special exhibit that is a favorite with children, visitors explore six larger than life habitats, or animal homes. They can climb up into a lifelike dinosaur named Daisy and make her roar, or walk beneath a beaver pond and view it as if they were in the water. In a giant beehive, they can smell honey and look out through a model of the

A summer festival at the art museum.

many parts of a bee's eye. Or they can observe the stages of a monarch butterfly—from a caterpillar crawling to a butterfly flying. At the center of the Treehouse, a four-story ficus (fig) tree rises and spreads its branches over the animals.

Scientists at the zoo observe the animals to see how they live in captivity and what they need to stay healthy. Years ago, zoo doctors discovered that monkeys could catch diseases from humans. They decided to move the monkeys behind glass walls to protect them from the germs of people. Since the zoo has a million visitors every year, the wall stops many human germs that could kill the monkeys.

Around the zoo, Fairmount Park spreads out over miles of the city. On summer nights, families come to hear free concerts in the open theater in the Robin Hood Dell. They sit on blankets under a starry sky, and enjoy jazz, rock and roll, or classical music.

When Fairmount Park was first planned more than one hundred years ago, the city made sure that it would be large enough to serve as a recreational, cultural, and nature center. Onto a map of Philadelphia the planners drew a park that branched out from Center City into many Philadelphia neighborhoods to the north and west.

At the Philadelphia Zoo, children watch a polar bear underwater through the windows below the surface of its tank.

4

A City of Neighborhoods

In Philadelphia, most of the neighborhoods have a history that reflects the people who have settled there. Today, each neighborhood has its own special character.

In Chestnut Hill, to the north and west of Center City, Germantown Avenue attracts local residents and visitors. Along the avenue, colonial signs hang outside of restaurants with names such as The Flying Fish, The Blushing Zebra, and Under the Blue Moon. Store windows display fine, hand-painted tiles, expensive silk gowns, wooden trains, watercolor paints, and potted geraniums. Every few minutes, a trolley clangs as it runs along the avenue.

In Chestnut Hill, people may live in large old houses with gingerbread trim. They also live in sparkling white farmhouses, or in stone man-

These girls are window-shopping on Germantown Avenue, Chestnut Hill's main street.

sions with turrets. Many of the houses have formal gardens tucked away in the back yards.

The first settlers in Chestnut Hill followed a muddy American Indian trail out of the Olde City. Because the new settlement was so beautiful, the path was soon rutted by carts carrying the belongings of other settlers. This path to Chestnut Hill was later named Germantown Avenue. The avenue connects Chestnut Hill to another well-known Philadelphia neighborhood, Germantown.

In William Penn's day, the people who lived in Germantown were mostly German. Today, the residents of this neighborhood come from a variety of races and ethnic groups.

Long ago, rich Philadelphians built summer homes in Germantown. They wanted to avoid yellow fever and other diseases that spread in hot weather in crowded Center City. Some of these great houses still stand. At one old mansion, Cliveden, visitors are shown where a musket ball sticks in the parlor wall. A guide tells them that during the Battle of Germantown in 1777, British soldiers fired on the house. The British won that Revolutionary War battle, and held Philadelphia for about a year before they were forced to retreat.

Many of the Germantown mansions are now divided into apartments which house several families. Yet, most residents of this neighborhood live in older row houses with front porches.

British soldiers fired on the Cliveden mansion during the Battle of Germantown.

Germantown is a short train ride from University City, across the Schuylkill River next to West Philadelphia. Drexel University, the University of Pennsylvania, and the University of Pennsylvania Hospital are located in this neighborhood.

Children who live in University City don't have to travel to Egypt to see real mummies. They can walk to the University Museum, where mummies in blackened wrappings lie behind glass. Here, they can see what the mummies once looked like from

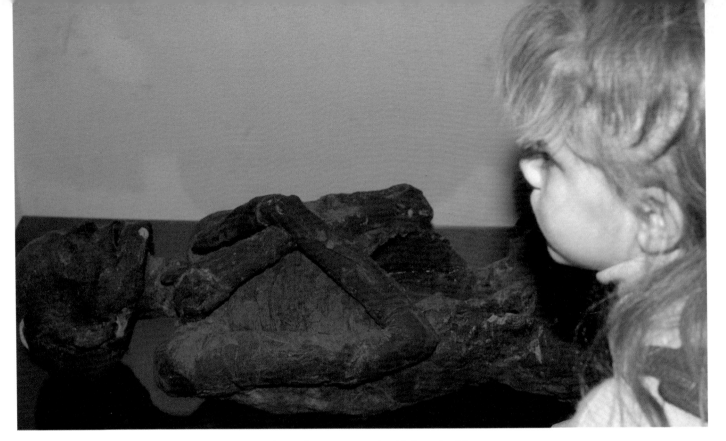

A young girl looks at the mummy in a glass case at the University Museum.

the faces painted on their gold coffins, called sarcophaguses.

The University Museum is only a short walk from another interesting place, the Civic Center Museum. In hands-on geography lessons, the teachers at this museum invite young people to pretend they live in other countries. For example, in a lesson on Latin America, children may grind the coffee beans that Central and South American farmers grow. In a lesson on Africa's nomadic tribes, they can dress in brown robes and

Guided by a teacher, children take part in a Japanese tea ceremony at the Civic Center Museum.

wrap their heads in turbans for an imaginary trip across the desert in a camel caravan.

University City, with its brownstone houses and university buildings, does not look much like its crosstown neighbor, Northeast Philadelphia. In the Northeast, blocks and blocks of row houses sit side by side.

During the 1950s and 1960s, Philadelphia grew rapidly, and needed more homes to house its new citizens. Northeast Philadelphia, once a land of rolling farms, quickly became an area of new housing developments. Today, most of the Northeast is made up of houses, industrial parks, schools, and shopping malls. This large area includes many neighborhoods, some old and some new.

A superhighway, called I-95, connects the neighborhoods of the Northeast. Along this interstate highway, travelers see the silver tanks of an enormous chemical company. At night, white lights gleam on the tall factory smokestacks of industries along the Delaware River.

Below the great concrete highway are several Philadelphia communities. One, Bridesburg, lies in the shadow of the factories that line the Delaware River. In Bridesburg, rows of brick houses face each other across tiny, narrow streets. The streets often serve as a playground for children, who toss their basketballs at hoops nailed to telephone poles. Sometimes, they have to stop their play to let cars drive through their court.

I-95 runs from North to South Philadelphia along the Delaware River. From the highway, riders can see some of the nearly 300 piers and terminals of the Port of Philadelphia. Huge steel cranes look like arms hanging out over the water. The cranes pluck cargo from ships that travel up the river from the Atlantic Ocean, carrying oil for the refineries and iron ore for the steel mills.

Each day in the port—one of the world's busiest—dockworkers unload freight for Philadelphia businesses. On strong ropes, they hoist cars from ship to shore for delivery to automobile showrooms. They unload big rolls of material for the clothing makers, and huge sacks of flour for the bakeries. The port's activity

Cargo ships line the Delaware River at the piers and terminals of the Port of Philadelphia.

extends along the Delaware River all the way from North to South Philadelphia.

Many Italians still live in South Philadelphia, an area that offers a great variety of tasty foods. On Saturdays, Philadelphians flock to the Italian Market on Ninth Street. There, shoppers jostle each other to reach their favorite stands, where they find everything from barrels of candy to grated cheese, olive oil, and fresh tomatoes. Smelly trucks idle in the one-way street as drivers slide wooden crates of vegetables under the stands. Under the striped awnings, shoppers haggle with vendors over the price of squid, sausages, and herbs.

A few blocks away from Ninth Street is a magical place called South Street. On this carnival-like street, anything goes. Teenagers in pink mohawk hairdos stroll beside gentlemen in suits. Families from Northeast Philadelphia mingle with families from India or Japan. Old jewelry and costumes, pottery and purple feathers— all are sold on South Street.

A South Street restaurant, painted bright pink and green, serves omelettes to its customers. Another restaurant, with tiny brass bells at its doorway, serves egg rolls and chow mein. Sidewalk cafés serve Philly cheesesteaks and soda. Music blares out of the stores.

In the parks of South Philadelphia, older men play bocce ball, a game taught to them by their Italian

Young people play hockey on a side street in South Philadelphia.

fathers and grandfathers. On the side streets, younger people play a newer game, hockey. Their roller skates scrape along the blacktop as the hockey players dive for the puck. Serious hockey players sign up for ice-hockey lessons at the local ice-skating rink.

The sports complex, where the professional teams play, stands in the middle of South Philadelphia. At the gates to Veterans Stadium, fans wait for autographs from the Philadelphia Phillies baseball stars or the Eagles football players. Nearby, at the doors

Many visitors come aboard the USS *Kitty Hawk* at the Philadelphia Naval Base.

to the Spectrum, basketball and hockey fans take photographs of their favorite Philadelphia 76er or Flyer.

Beside the Delaware River in South Philadelphia is a United States navy base. Docked at the base is a famous aircraft carrier, the USS *Kitty Hawk*. In active service during the Vietnam War, the ship now serves as a kind of floating naval museum. On field trips, South Philadelphia scout troops and their leaders climb the ship's iron stairs to visit the captain's quarters. From there, they look down

on a giant runway where planes can take off and land.

Those who explore the *Kitty Hawk* will hear planes flying over their heads. But these planes are headed for another runway, a short distance down the river from the navy base, at Philadelphia International Airport. The airport marks the southern boundary of Philadelphia.

The jets fly out past the Tinicum Wildlife Preserve, where white-tail deer run from the loud engine noises. Ducks float in the marshes of the preserve, and muskrats hide among the reeds.

On a clear day, passengers in a plane leaving International Airport may catch a glimpse of Center City. If they look closely, they may see the statue of William Penn rising above City Hall. The soaring statue reminds Philadelphians of the hopes and dreams of those who founded the City of Brotherly Love.

Places to Visit in Philadelphia

Academy of Natural Sciences Museum
19th Street and Benjamin Franklin Parkway
(215) 299-1000

Betsy Ross House
Arch Street between 2nd and 3rd streets
(215) 627-5343

Carpenters' Hall
Independence National Historical Park
Chestnut Street between 3rd and 4th
streets
(215) 925-0167
*Building where the First Continental Congress
was held.*

Christ Church Burial Ground
Independence National Historical Park
5th and Arch streets
(215) 597-8974
Burial place of Revolutionary War leaders.

City Hall
Broad and Market streets
(215) 567-4476

Civic Center Museum
34th Street and Civic Center Boulevard
(215) 823-7400

Cliveden
6401 Germantown Avenue
(215) 848-1777
Country house and site of the Battle of Germantown.

Fairmount Park Trolley Bus
Philadelphia Visitors Center
16th Street and John F. Kennedy Boulevard
(215) 636-1666
*See also Independence National Historical
Park Visitors Center.*

Franklin Court
Independence National Historical Park
Market Street between 3rd and 4th streets
(215) 597-8974
*Includes a working printing office and bindery,
museum, and the Franklin Post Office.*

Franklin Institute Science Museum
20th Street and Benjamin Franklin Parkway
(215) 448-1200
Includes the Fels Planetarium (extension 1292).

The Gallery at Market East
9th and Market streets
(215) 925-7162

Graff House
Independence National Historical Park
7th and Market streets
(215) 597-8974
Building where Thomas Jefferson wrote the Declaration of Independence.

Independence Hall
Independence National Historical Park
5th and Chestnut streets
(215) 597-8974

Independence National Historical Park
Visitors Center
3rd and Chestnut streets
(215) 597-8974
Trolley bus tours and other information about famous historical sites.

Liberty Bell Pavilion
Independence National Historical Park
Market Street between 5th and 6th streets
(215) 597-8974

Mummers Museum
2nd and Washington streets
(215) 336-3050

Penn's Landing
Delaware Avenue between Market and Spruce streets
(215) 923-8181

Philadelphia Museum of Art
26th Street and Benjamin Franklin Parkway
(215) 763-8100

Philadelphia Visitors Center
16th Street and John F. Kennedy Boulevard
(215) 636-1666

Philadelphia Zoo
34th Street and Girard Avenue
(215) 243-1100

Please Touch Museum for Children
210 N. 21st Street
(215) 963-0666 or 0667

United States Mint
5th and Arch streets
(215) 597-7350

University Museum
University of Pennsylvania
33rd and Spruce streets
(215) 898-4000

Additional information can be obtained from these agencies:

Independence National Historical Park
Visitors Center
3rd and Chestnut streets
Philadelphia, PA 19106
(215) 597-8974

Philadelphia Convention and Visitors
Bureau
1515 Market Street
Philadelphia, PA 19102
(215) 636-3300

Philadelphia: A Historical Time Line

1682   William Penn founds Philadelphia

1688   First public protest against slavery, organized by German Quakers, takes place in Germantown at home of Thomas Kunder

1689   William Penn Charter School is founded

1723   Benjamin Franklin arrives in Philadelphia

1740   Delaware Valley becomes a shipbuilding center

1774   First Continental Congress meets at Carpenters' Hall

1776   Declaration of Independence is first read in public; Betsy Ross designs the first American flag

1777-78 British occupy Philadelphia during the Revolutionary War

1787   United States Constitution is signed

1790-1800 Philadelphia is capital of United States

1792   Mint is established by Act of Congress

1818   Philadelphia Public School district is established

1876   Centennial Exposition, held in Fairmount Park, celebrates one hundredth anniversary of the United States

1890   Roman Catholic High School, first free parochial high school in country, opens

1925   Benjamin Franklin Bridge is built across the Delaware River

1927   Free Library of Philadelphia is built

1942   First computer developed at Moore School, University of Pennsylvania

1976   United States Bicentennial Celebration is held in Philadelphia

1983   Wilson Goode is elected as Philadelphia's first black mayor

1987   Tallest building in Philadelphia, One Liberty Place, changes the city skyline; two hundredth anniversary of the United States Constitution is celebrated in Philadelphia

1988   King Carl XVI Gustaf and Queen Silvia of Sweden visit Philadelphia—site of the first American school, built by Swedes in 1638—to celebrate 350 years of friendship between Sweden and the United States

Index